About the aut

Mary Lunnen is a life coach, facilitator, and currently works part time for a local college as a business adviser and trainer. She began writing at an early age and became passionate about 'words for well-being' the day she was diagnosed with cancer in 1994.

The journal she started that day became a compilation of women's stories, published as *Flying in the Face of Fear* in 1998. Since then Mary has had a number of articles published in magazines and papers ranging from *The Craftsman* to the *Western Morning News*, and has contributed to *Prompted to Write* – a compilation of accounts of workshops run in Cornwall by Lapidus.

Dare to Blossom Life Coaching was launched in 2003, and Mary works with people wanting to achieve their potential and love the lives they live. Mary coaches on the telephone and face-to-face, and runs inspirational workshops on the theme of coaching and creativity

Mary lives in the country in Cornwall with her husband and always at least one cat. She welcomes visitors to her website www.daretoblossom.co.uk.

Other books by Mary Lunnen

Flying in the Face of Fear: surviving cervical cancer (1998)

Contributed to: Prompted to Write (2007)

Dare to Blossom
Creativity and Coaching

Mary Lunnen

Dare to Blossom Books
Cornwall

Dedication

In loving memory of my mother, Joan Nunn,
who taught me to keep smiling and never to give up.

Acknowledgements

Thank you to all the people who have inspired and helped me over the years. All the writers mentioned in my references, and many more along the way. The teachers, therapists, friends and everyone who has passed through my life have all had their part to play. The connections and interlinking of our lives is a continual joy, whether a brief conversation by email or a longer-lasting friendship.

Thank you to the people who have come to me for coaching or attended workshops, every one of you has brought me a special gift. Thank you to Liz and Anna for writing so openly about your thoughts and feelings. Without my own life coach, Fraser Dyer, I would not be writing this now, I will always be grateful to you. In relation to the publication of this book, many thanks to my volunteer readers: Christine Lewis, Diane Eardley, Jacky Pratt, and Claire Cohen. You have all contributed invaluable feedback and advice. Thank you to all my family, near and far. Thank you to my husband Dave for your love, support and patience, not to mention proof reading. My love and appreciation to you all.

Contents

A bout this book

I firmly believe that when you are drawn to a book like this it is for a reason – so welcome and thank you for reading this. There will be something between these covers that is a message for you – it might be the whole book, a chapter, or a single line that shines a light for you on your way ahead.

I am fascinated to know how you found your way to this book and what made you order it online or pick it up in a bookshop. For me, writing is a powerful magic whereby I first distil thoughts out of the jumble of my own mind, then set them down on paper, and perhaps rearrange and polish them a little. Then they are sent out into the unknown as a newsletter, a response to a coaching question, a magazine article or a book. Now you are reading these words, my trust is that you will find a nugget of inspiration for your path in life.

The book is in two parts. The main section is a series of short chapters on different topics. Some of them contain well-known life coaching exercises, others are accounts of how I have used various techniques myself. The intention is to offer you ideas and for you to choose any that appeal to you. You might want to read it straight through, to work through it doing the exercises in order, or to dip in and out. There is a list of the exercises at the end of the book so you can find a particular one easily.

To make the exercises as useful as possible it is good to prepare first. Make sure that you have at least half an hour when you will not be disturbed. Perhaps put the answerphone on, and ask the family not to interrupt.

Find a notebook and pen – you might like to buy a special book for this where you can keep all your notes and exercises as you work through this book. It can be interesting, and sometimes illuminating to look back some time later at how you were feeling. One of my clients has a special pink book to write her journal in and a pink ring binder to keep all her exercises together.

Sit somewhere comfortable, put some soft music on if that is good for you. Then relax, if you want you could do a yoga relaxation such as tensing and relaxing each part of your body. Clear your mind as much as possible. Tell yourself that this time is just for you, put all your thoughts and worries in a metaphorical box and leave it outside of the door where you can pick them up again later (or not, they may have disappeared or become irrelevant).

This way of preparing will be helpful for all of the exercises in this book. The more you can feel relaxed and open to your own inner knowing about what is right and true for you, the more useful and illuminating the exercises will be for you. Having said all this – if time is limited, just find yourself somewhere peaceful, a pen and paper and get going!

One of the key principles of life coaching is that it is all about the person being coached. The approach taken, the exercises suggested, and particularly the questions asked are all tailored to suit that particular individual.

So, there could be a risk in describing examples from particular clients, or of how I have approached these exercises for myself. If you are a very practical business-like person, and you open this book on a page when I am discussing imagination, creative writing, following my intuition etc, you may feel that it is not for you.

Please read further: there are other parts of this book that talk about setting goals, business plans and projections, the sort of thing that a person of artistic temperament may feel they are not in tune with.

Aiming to attain balance in life applies internally within ourselves as well as externally. So, as well as balancing work and play; exercise and relaxation; family and friends; we may also benefit from balancing different aspects of our own characters: artistic, creative, practical, business-like, spiritual, light-hearted, serious, and so on. When I teach artistic people to draw up a cashflow forecast, they feel a huge sense of achievement once they have got through the numbers barrier. When practical, logical people attend a workshop and allow themselves to play with making things for no good reason at all, they laugh and have fun like children. Coaching is a process that can be applied to any situation.

The second part of this volume contains reflections on my journey "from cancer to coaching" answering the questions people have asked me about "what happened next?" after the end of my last book. After the publication of *Flying in the Face of Fear* in 1998, many people wrote or emailed about their own experiences. I would again be delighted to hear from any readers who would like to share their responses, thoughts or experiences. Finally, the details of any books that I have mentioned are given in the "References and Resources" section at the end of the book.

To finish this section, here is a quote from a client, Liz Scambler, a successful businesswoman:

"I needed a life coach but I never knew it, I often wondered what they did, it was one of those things I kept hearing about and thought it sounded a bit airy fairy and certainly not for me – after all I had what I wanted, knew where I was going and felt pretty much I had all angles covered! But then it all changed, I had the chance of a free session and wanted to try it, the more I looked into it the more tempted I became until I took the plunge and haven't looked back. Mary has been fantastic and although my course hasn't finished I am already forward planning to work out a way forward with her support. So for all of you who don't think life coaching is for you- try it and you might be surprised!"

Introduction

Part 1: The starting point: Daring to Blossom

These words were written in January 2007:

"I have been trying to start this book for a long time. I kept telling myself (in the words of one of my clients) 'if you want to be a writer, you have to write.' So I've written – my journal, letters, emails, work reports, shopping lists, to-do lists – everything but making a start on this book.

Today I am finally here and ready, and have decided to work on the principle that 'a journey of a thousand miles starts with a single step.' So this book, which I hope will contain many thousand words, starts with a single page, or a single word: DARE."

I have been daring myself to blossom for a few years now, and in the manner of a timid child (and that child definitely lives within me still), I've been hiding behind the sofa, peeking between my fingers, anything but daring to stand up and blossom into the full glory of my true self.

When I started my business I was inspired by the Anais Nin quote "..and then the day came when the risk to remain tight in a bud was more painful than the risk it took to blossom." I tracked down the publisher's agent in the USA and obtained permission to use the quote on my publicity material.

The Anais Nin quote is about moving away from pain, the other thing that motivates us to take action is moving towards pleasure. Creativity is often seen as both pain and pleasure. The pain of deciding what to write, paint or create; the irritation of all the barriers we put in our own way; the guilt of the delaying tactics. The pleasure of sitting down and making something out of nothing; the joy of expressing ourselves; the excitement of finding out about ourselves and our way of viewing the world; the satisfaction of being able to pass that on in some way to other people.

One reason for writing this book is to share some of the experiences and insights I have had since I wrote the story of my cancer journey. Looking back I know that what at the time was a terrible event was the doorway to a new life. I have met wonderful people and learnt to value every minute of every day. I have learnt new things about myself, the world, the universe.

The second reason is to introduce you to the simple but powerful process of life coaching that can enable you to take charge of your own life and dare to blossom. Over the time that this book took to develop, I found this becoming the main focus for this book. I now plan to write another telling my own story in more detail.

Part 2: Coaching and Creativity

I decided the sub-title would include "coaching and creativity" not long after I began running *Awaken your creativity* workshops. These have had some astonishing results. Taking a day away from our normal surroundings to play with different ideas and actually make something from unusual materials can be a transformational process.

Anna Colmer, a zero-balancing practitioner who has become a good friend, wrote the following reflection six months later:

"I did a workshop with Mary, back in the Spring, and had a really enjoyable and constructive day. I met some lovely women and a lot of very affirming female bonding went on."

"I also got clearer about some of my priorities and, best of all, rediscovered my creativity which had been lying dormant for a very long time.... Mary presents and facilitates with lightness and humour and a degree of personal honesty which is very refreshing. I'd particularly recommend the workshop if you are in transition, feeling stuck or have unfulfilled dreams. You have nothing to lose, everything to gain and I can promise you an inspiring and thought-provoking day."

For a while the workshops seemed in some way separate from the one to one coaching work that I do. Recently, though, the two have been coming together in a way that was probably obvious but not so for me to begin with.

Coaching is about enabling people to recognise where they are now and plan where they want to go next in their lives. Some people come to me having already identified very clear goals, others just know that they are not happy or satisfied with their lives and want to do things differently. My approach is to work with each person to uncover their own knowing about themselves and how to allow themselves to shine and achieve their fullest possible potential.

Creativity is using the imagination to create something. This is precisely what I am doing in my coaching work. I am enabling people to see clearly what they want in life and visualise what it will be like, i.e. using their imagination to create it.

Everything starts with a thought: every action, every invention, every written word, every piece of art, every conversation. Everything we do in life is about creating.

For me personally the breakthrough was becoming consciously aware that this is the case, and that we all have a choice about what we create through our thoughts. We create *unconsciously* all the time. For example, I may wake up in the morning feeling grumpy and tired because I haven't slept well. I get up and snap at my husband because of this, so then he gets cross, I feel bad about it and feel cross too.... I have begun to create a bad day for both of us if we let it be so.

I have learnt that I can take responsibility for creating my own day and also helping to make things better for others. (Though they, too, must take responsibility for themselves).

One of the angel cards I use regularly for reflection says: "Education: Cultivate your ability to learn from life's rich patterns. You may not be able to establish the curriculum, but you can elect what courses to take at any given time and how to apply your knowledge."[1] In other words, you cannot always choose what happens in life, but you can choose how to respond.

I feel that "Daring to Blossom" is all about connection: with our inner selves, our true selves, and with others in a real, genuine way. It is about being brave enough to say "This is who I am right now, in this moment. Who are you? How can we connect?" We might not use those words, but being able to be our true selves leads to true connection with the people we are drawn to at the various stages of our lives.

Coaching and being coached **is** a creative activity. It does not need to be complicated. Coaching helps you to become clear on what you want in your life. The clearer your goal or target is, the more likely you are to achieve it. Coaching also helps you identify and consider all the possible routes to achieving your goals. Therefore, if you find one route is blocked, another may still be open.

When someone decides to use life coaching to enable them to move forward they are making a

---

[1] 'The Angel Cards Book', Kathy Tyler and Joy Drake

decision to take an active part in creating a new life for themselves.

Some further definitions:

Life Coaching

Coaching is a professional service providing clients with feedback, insights, and guidance from an outside vantage point. Coaching is an on-going collaborative partnership built on taking action. People hire a life coach when they are making a career transition, starting a new business, feeling dissatisfied, re-evaluating life choices, or looking for personal and professional breakthroughs.

Creativity

The Oxford English Dictionary[2] defines the word creative, as: "adjective involving the use of the imagination or original ideas in order to create something." The derivatives being: creatively (adverb), creativeness (noun), and creativity (noun).

Many of us believe that we are not "creative" people, and maybe that people who are creative are somehow different. There is the popular vision of

---

[2] I used the online dictionary at www.askoxford.com

artists as troubled people, struggling, even "starving in a garret", unkempt, unsociable, even dependent on drink or drugs. Why would we want to be like that?! At other times we may see artists as being very successful people with exhibitions all over the world that may seem equally unrelated to us.

However, we are all creating all the time without even trying. Our bodies are processing food, water and air to produce new cells and to keep us functioning physically and mentally. Our minds are creating thoughts and ideas that affect how we experience the world around us. Our actions create physical things: from a nourishing meal to a revolutionary invention. Everything made by human beings began with an idea in someone's mind.

We are literally the creators of our own world. So, it follows that we can choose what kind of world to create. Even when we are affected by external events and circumstances we can choose how we respond to those external influences. This is the case even in the most extreme circumstances. The famous book *Man's Search for Meaning* by Viktor E. Frankl is an extraordinary account of his experiences in a concentration camp. Frankl learnt that no matter what was taken from him, he still retained control over his choice of response to his circumstances.

The life coaching work I do with people one-to-one and in workshops revolves around this. The coaching process helps you gain clarity about your life now, about what you can change and what you cannot. Then you can identify options and go on to make choices about the path you wish to take towards the goals you are aiming for – and you are creating your future.

Almost a year after I wrote the words at the beginning of this Introduction, the shape and content of this book has finally become clear. It feels as if the end of this journey is near, another doorway is opening as I ready my work to go out into the world.

C hapter 1: Reviewing where you are now and where you want to be

In order to make changes it is necessary to know where you are now and where you want to be. Thinking in terms of maps: if you do not know where you are in life, how can you first of all "find yourself" and then make a plan to change how things are for you?

Taking stock helps gain clarity. Many of us continue on in our daily lives hardly pausing to think, let alone review what is happening to us.

Exercise: Life balance

One of the first exercises many coaches offer their clients is some variation on the Wheel of Life exercise. Here is one version for you to try. It will show you very graphically if your life is out of balance in any area.

The wheel of life exercise allows you to determine whether you are focusing too much on one part of your life and so neglecting other parts. The wheel is divided into sections. You can draw your own wheel on a piece of paper and you can change the headings as you wish, or add more.

Regarding the centre of the wheel as 0 and the outer edge as 10, rank your level of satisfaction with each life area by drawing a straight or curved line to create a new outer edge. The new perimeter of the circle represents the Wheel of Life. How bumpy would the ride be if this were a real wheel?

Your wheel shows you the degree to which you are satisfied with your level of balance in your life. Which are your low spots – the areas you are least satisfied with? Make a list of them and rank them in order of importance to you right now. Taking rank number 1 – the areas of your life you are least satisfied with, answer the following questions:

- What can I do personally to improve things?
- What can I ask others to do?
- How will I know that things have improved – what will I feel, see and hear that is different and better?
- How much do I really want to achieve more satisfaction with this particular area?

I regularly do this exercise for myself and it is always useful. It allows me to refocus on what is actually happening in my life now.

Exercise: Your ideal day

Now that you have some ideas about what you would like to change in your life, try looking at things from another angle. What would it be like if your life was perfectly in balance? How would things be for you? What would you be doing? What would the structure of your days be like?

An exercise to help with this is to write about "My ideal day." This would be a typical day, perhaps working in your home or away from it, or both; caring for children; doing all the normal things. To make this as useful as possible it is good to prepare first, as described in the "About this book" chapter.

Write about your ideal day. Imagine it in as much detail as possible: where will you wake up? How will you feel? Who will be with you? What will you see when you open your eyes? What will you be looking forward to doing that day? Think about what you will experience with all your senses: what will you see, hear, touch, taste, or smell? As you get out of bed and put your feet on the floor, what will be there? A luxurious long-pile carpet? A fluffy rug on a beautifully polished floor?

When you open the curtains what will you see? A garden full of flowers? A scenic view of river, sea, mountains, countryside, or forest?

As you get dressed what will you wear? Who will you speak to? You walk out of your bedroom, what does your house look like? What do you smell? The scent of a vase of flowers? Fresh coffee brewing? Perhaps bread baking? Do you hear your children playing happily? Your cat purring as you stroke her silky fur?

Paint as vivid a picture as you can for yourself, bringing in touch, smell, hearing, taste, sight. As you get ready for the day you catch a glimpse of yourself in a big mirror, you look happy, radiant and glowing.

Carry on imagining the day to come, whether you will go out, what you will do. Are you going to work? What is that like? Imagine the surroundings there in detail as you did for your house.

Work right through the day, to the evening where you relax at after a good meal. (What did that taste like, look like, feel like as you put the spoon of fresh strawberries and clotted cream in your mouth?).

Keep going and don't edit or censor yourself, this is to free your mind from the restrictive thoughts we usually imprison ourselves with. Any time that worries and thoughts about 'real life' come into your mind, put them aside again, tell them that you are busy!

You can repeat this process any time you wish. Perhaps varying it to a week day when you are going out to work, a weekend with the family, a day on holiday, etc.

You may feel this is daydreaming. Yes, it is! But as has long been recognised, dreaming is the first stage of creation.

"What the mind of man can conceive and believe, he can achieve." This was written by Napoleon Hill, writing after the Great Depression in the 1930s in his book *Think and Grow Rich*.

An example close to my heart is the Eden Project, here in Cornwall – few people could have believed that the dream of Tim Smit and the other members of his team would be achieved in such spectacular fashion.

You may find that you meet people who can help you (apparently by coincidence), or who give you useful tips and ideas. This is partly because, having made the decision and the commitment, you are looking out for these things, whereas beforehand you might not have seen them at all. This leads on to the topic of Chapter 2, Opportunities.

C hapter 2: Opportunities

Now you have some ideas about what you would like to change in your life to get it in balance and about how you would like to be spending your days in your ideal world, how do you set about creating some of those things in your life?

Exercise: Opportunities

You are probably already thinking about what you could do. Try this exercise to help focus your thoughts.

Take a piece of paper and draw a line down the centre. On the left hand side write "What" and on the right hand side "How".

To encourage a flow of writing, it can be helpful to fold the paper in half down the line so you are looking at only the "What" column to start with.

Write a list of all the things you want to achieve. It might look a bit like one of those lists of "100 things to do before you get old" – that is fine, but it need not be like that. Keep going, don't allow that internal editor or censor to pipe up saying "that's

20

silly, you're too old, too fat, too thin, too scared, too poor," etc.

When you have written down everything you can think of, open the page out. There are two ways of doing the next step.

1. Straight away go down through your list and write something in the "How" column next to each item.

2. Alternatively, you may prefer to organise the "What" list into some sort of priority first (here it can be easier to do it on the computer so you can cut and paste, but can be done on paper with a new sheet). The order might be "most important" to you first, or it might be "easiest to achieve". Or you might mix these up, perhaps one "easy to achieve", followed by a "most important".

Either way, the magic of this process is that once you start you might find the boundaries blurring – the important things may not be hard to achieve after all.

Then, *do something!* Although I have been making the point that everything people achieve starts with an idea in their mind, nothing will happen unless they take action. This might be asking someone for help, making a phone call, doing some research, going for a walk, applying for a job. Whatever it is, the first stage is going through the process of deciding that it is the right action for you to take now. Choosing what you are going to do or how you will respond to events means that you are in control.

If you start to feel stuck with your lists, put them aside for a few days or even weeks and come back to them with fresh eyes.

A quote: "That the moment one definitely commits oneself, then providence moves, too." (often attributed to Goethe, apparently from W. H. Murray[3]). This is not only about you committing yourself to the action, it also brings in providence or the universe – the idea that you set in movement a train of events by making a clear decision.

Exercise: Create a vision board

After lots of thinking and writing, you could now try something really visual and hands on. Find a piece of strong cardboard or plywood, perhaps a pin

---

[3] *The Scottish Himalya Expedition 1951*

board, as big as possible. Collect together lots of materials, for example:

Old magazines, birthday or Christmas cards

Scissors

Coloured paper

Glue or pins

Paint or brightly coloured felt-tip pens

Favourite photographs of people (including yourself) and places

Shiny shapes, stars, butterflies etc, glitter, feathers, pressed flowers

Etc, etc!

Choose or make images drawn from your "Ideal Day" and "What" exercises and start fixing them on your board to make a colourful collage of what you want your future to be like. So it could be a picture of the sort of person you visualise as your ideal partner – or perhaps some of their qualities e.g. a red heart for romance, a pair of holding hands etc.

An important note here, one of the principles in this type of work on creating your own future is to always add in your mind "for the greatest good of all concerned." So for example, it would not be right to concentrate on having a particular person as your partner irrespective of the effects on their existing partner and family, or to wish for something that involved depriving the rightful owner of their property.

The principle of abundance states that there is always enough for everyone, always a partner you have not yet met, - as long as having those things is "for the greatest good."

This exercise is great fun for children to do and can lead to some wonderful discussions about what is important to them, which in their turn may prompt us adults to think more deeply about our priorities too.

This exercise can be adapted in various ways, you might want to do it each New Year to think about what you want to achieve in the year ahead. Taking out the previous year's collage or picture can be illuminating. You may find you have achieved many of the things there, perhaps not in an obvious way. You may also found that the things that did not come to pass are no longer important to you, or even that you are glad they did not happen!

Chapter 3: Anticipation

When I decide to use a word as a title I find it useful and often inspiring to look it up first. One dictionary definition is: "Anticipation: noun, the action of anticipating; expectation or prediction; a prior action that takes into account or forestalls a later action."

To me this can be about the balance between creating our own future, as we have been looking at in the last two chapters, and letting the process take place without attachment or "anticipation" of how it will work. Sometimes our expectations of what will happen lead us to overlook the reality of what is happening.

I have attended talks by Jack Russell at several conferences. He involves the audience actively in various parts of his presentation (including getting a volunteer to break a plank of wood with their hand – but that is another story!)

In one of them he tricks the brains of those in the audience through having them repeatedly read aloud in unison: "red, green, red, green....", (though those words are written on the screen in the opposite colours), into answering the question "what do you do at a green light?", with "STOP!" (see the References section for his excellent book *Don't tell the bumblebee.*)

Sometimes we anticipate too much, and may worry about things that have not (and never will!) happen. Mark Twain wrote: "I am an old man and have known a great many troubles, but most of them never happened." There is more about this in Chapter 5 where we look at negative self-talk.

On a positive note, good anticipation, in other words good preparation, can instil confidence. For example, risk assessment is all about looking at all possible risks and putting in place measures to reduce or deal with them. Once that is done it is possible to relax and enjoy the activity in the knowledge that those measures are in place if anything did happen.

Another dictionary defines anticipation as: "expectant waiting - the feeling of looking forward, usually excitedly or eagerly, to something that is going to happen."

What are you "waiting expectantly" for? Can you remember that feeling as a child of waiting for

Christmas, your birthday, the summer holidays? How about when those events arrived? Were you disappointed?

Many of us feel similar emotions looking forward to acquiring new things, a car, house, new clothes. Often, however, once we have them we feel a sense of anti-climax, of "now what?", and wondering why our lives are not happier and more fulfilled. So the next exercise might help if you are not sure what to put on your vision board, or if the one you have done has not felt true to you when you came back to it.

Exercise: Feelings and exploring "what I really want"

Take a new sheet of paper or page in your notebook and on the left hand side write a list of all the things you are waiting for, e.g.: the new house, more money, a better job, the ideal relationship, a perfectly shaped nose. Keep going, put down everything you have ever wanted or wished you could have.

When you have the longest possible list, look at each item and decide what feeling you think you would have when you obtained that item. So, the new house might be: security, comfort, space. The ideal relationship: love, security, being wanted.

Look through this list when you have finished and write a new one of the feelings you have identified. You may find the list of feelings is much shorter. This time, on the right hand side of the page, write a heading 'what this will do for me' and against each feeling answer that question. Keep looking deeper each time until you reach one or a few key feelings or qualities that you truly desire.

The final step in this exercise is to write about how you already receive these feelings in your life. At some stage the realisation will come to you that they are present in some form: you may be failing to recognise them, just not noticing they are there. If you feel you do not have anything prompting the desired feelings, how can you bring them into your life, even in a small way?

For example, when I did this exercise, I wrote that I was waiting for: "time to rest", and it would bring me peace and enjoyment. But who was stopping me taking time to rest? Me! I could make "more time" in various ways: I could choose to spend less time looking at emails; I could practise saying "no" more often; not take on so much for other people. I could have time to rest, to give me those feelings of peace and enjoyment, if I wanted it enough to take action to make it happen.

I also realised that even when I did plan activities that would bring me those desired feelings, so often I did not enjoy the pleasurable anticipation I spoke of earlier. Even when I got to my time of sitting quietly reading or another relaxing activity – I often spoilt it for myself by feeling guilty for taking that time for myself!

I am well aware that as human beings we are all "practising" during our personal growth and development and in my career as a life coach I am dealing with the same issues as everyone else. In the old truism of plumbers having leaking taps and mechanics having cars needing fixing, I find myself as imperfectly human as all my clients. My own life coach, Fraser, makes me laugh by saying "Well Mary, if you were your own client what would you say to yourself?" And I ruefully reply, "Yes I *know* but it is hard to actually do it!"

The core of this exercise is that having said we are all "imperfectly human", the other part of us is already a whole, complete, perfect being. If we can persuade our ego to step aside and allow our deeper knowing and intuition a chance to step in – as in my example above where I realised that I could already "make" time to rest – we can find ways of achieving the feeling we want now without waiting.

Chapter 4: Energy and Evolution

Now you have the list of feelings, can you use them to create more energy for yourself, a forward momentum? Every so often I think we all get a feeling of being stuck, not moving, even repeating the same patterns. I know I do. A while ago I wrote the article below for my newsletter about waiting for the "flow":

Mud flats – and the incoming tide

Reflections: written on a warm late summer day, sitting by the mud flats near the Camel Trail. (If you are not familiar with N Cornwall, this is a cycle track along the old railway line alongside the River Camel, though the vision of camel trekking is an attractive mental picture!)

I am looking up a creek away from the main river estuary. I can see an ancient landscape of fields, trees, hedges, and the salt marshes that are only occasionally covered by the highest tides. It is low tide now and the mud flats are exposed with streams cutting winding channels through them. The mud looks glutinous and smelly, but it is full of life, little worms and shellfish. The bigger pools have grey mullet swimming in them, splashing occasionally – though I can't see them swimming beneath the surface as the water is murky. A breeze stirs the surface of the water; the tide has turned and is coming in steadily.

I feel sometimes that my plans and ideas are lost in a murky, muddy morass. I can't see clearly what I should do next, or which way to go. Some of the steps I take feel like wading in the deep sticky mud.

Maybe I just need to wait for the tide to turn, in its own time – nothing I can do will speed it up. Once the tide covers the mud flats new life will sweep in, free to swim and feed and breed in a big expanse of open water.

The book I am working on has felt bogged down recently. I have been feeling that I have been working away at it but not getting anywhere. Some new ideas have just started emerging in my mind, maybe the tide is changing and I will soon find the right words.

Is there something you are trying to do that feels "stuck" or "bogged down"? Are you being too impatient? Would waiting for the "tide" – of ideas, of the seasons, of fashion or trends – to change make all the difference? If things you are trying to do seem difficult, a struggle, are you trying to "swim against the tide"? If you choose your time will the tide carry you along with it and take you where you need to go?

I thought about these questions and found the insights helpful: maybe I had been trying to swim against the tide, struggling against the current. If I relaxed and "went with the flow" my perspective would change and I would reach new understandings. I used this reflection to help me be patient in working on this book, and to give the process of writing the time it needs.

I have learnt that my cycles of energy and progression (or evolution) mirror the cycles of nature. Sometimes literally with the seasons, sometimes to my own rhythm. I have times when I need to rest, reflect, recover my energy. This can be equivalent to the winter when nature lies dormant. The plants and trees may appear dead and infertile, but all the while their buds are developing, bulbs growing, seeds germinating, hidden from sight. Once conditions are right for each individual plant, perhaps in early spring or later in the early summer, the sap rises, the buds break, the flower shoots burst forth in new growth and blossom.

In my life I have observed that even when I seem to be repeating experiences, mistakes even, when I look closely there is a progression, an evolution. A spiral of experience as I grow and learn. I know now that I need to be conscious of these repetitions, and learn from them. If I want to avoid them coming round again, I can by fully observing (and learning and acting on) the lesson. There are lots of wise truisms about this, such as: "If you keep thinking the way you've always thought, you'll keep doing what you've always done, and keep getting what you've always got."

And Einstein said: "We can't solve problems by using the same kind of thinking we used when we created them."

Exercise: Generating energy from feelings

Over to you: using your list of feelings from the last exercise, choose one to start with and write for fifteen minutes about it with the intention of exploring how you can use the energy of that feeling to move you upwards in your individual spiral of evolution. Use the free flow method of writing. Time yourself and do not read or censor what you write, just let the words flow out onto the paper. It does not matter what you write, (it might be "I don't know what to write."), simply keep going. When you have finished read through what you have written and underline or highlight key phrases or lines. You may like to note these separately or simply leave them "be", to see what else evolves from them.

When I did this myself again while writing this chapter I chose "freedom" as my feeling to write about. After writing for fifteen minutes and reading it

34

back, the phrase I underlined was: "Freedom of thought – not to be afraid of my thoughts." That definitely needed to be left to be and evolve.

Later I decided it would help to write about these questions. "Why freedom?", "What for?", and, "What will this do for me?" The answer that came up was, freedom to be me, the real me, all the different "me's", that are hidden away a lot of the time. I feel I have a lot more to work through on this for myself. On that occasion I didn't even start to think about "not to be afraid of my thoughts" – which would generate a whole new series of questions to reflect on. Your work with this exercise may be similar in the way it changes and evolves each time you come back to it.

How does this tie in with creating energy for ourselves? In this context it is to do with knowing ourselves better. In my example above, the realisation was that most of the time it is only me stopping myself being "free to be me". So the forward momentum I gain from this is: stop being afraid of my thoughts, take due consideration for others but not *undue* consideration. In other words: get on and do things once I am clear that it is right for me and what I really want.

Back to the dictionary once again:

Energy: noun (pl. energies)

1 the strength and vitality required for sustained activity.

2 (energies) a person's physical and mental powers as applied to a particular activity.

Origin: Greek *energeia*, from *ergon* 'work'.

It is interesting that the word "energy" derives from the word for "work". We tend to think of work as "using" energy, not as "being" energy. Perhaps if we look at it this way it can change our perception of work as something difficult, hard, dull, and as using up energy. The most satisfying types of work are those that do energise us, help us feel full of life and enthusiasm and the joy of living. Those activities that help us grow and evolve and develop to our highest potential.

So, in my example, how can I use the energy of being clear that it is my choice to allow myself to experience freedom? In a very practical way, I can use it to motivate myself to put dates in my diary for myself that are as binding as a work appointment or a lunch date with a friend. It is up to me to choose to keep "dates" with myself, give myself permission to take time for rest, reading, or any other activity.

A final quote to end this chapter: "It is not because things are difficult that we do not dare; it is because we do not dare that they are difficult." (Seneca: Roman dramatist, philosopher and politician.)

Using the energy generated by clarity of thought and intention clears away the difficulties we put in our own way, and us to achieve the outcomes we have dared to dream.

C hapter 5: Compassion and change

What have these two qualities to do with each other? I feel that I have paired them together to remind us that when making big changes it can be useful (vital in fact) to remember to have compassion for ourselves. I know I am much more critical of myself than anyone else would ever be. I give myself a hard time for every little mistake. As for a big one, well, I *never* let myself hear the end of it! Or that used to be how it was.

You may have heard the expression "negative self-talk". Take a metaphorical step back and listen to how you talk to yourself (mostly in your head silently, though, like me you may occasionally find yourself doing it out loud). You will hear an endless stream of mostly junk thoughts: "What shall I get for dinner? That's a nice dress. I wish I was as thin as her. Oh what a fool I am for stubbing my toe. I am a stupid idiot.….etc."

You have just said something to yourself that you would probably feel really bad saying to someone else. You may have done something stupid (though stubbing your toe is more likely a minor accident),

38

but that does not make you an idiot. (An aside to this is that if you listen to how you speak to your closest family you may also be horrified at how you treat them at times.)

The more we allow this stream of negative and self-critical thinking to continue unchecked, the lower our view of ourselves sinks. We don't expect anyone else to respect us or admire us because we do not respect or admire ourselves.

Exercise: Compassion and reducing negative self-talk

Try, for just one day, noticing how often you say negative things to yourself. You may well find that after a very short while it becomes impossible to keep count of how many times you do this. Once you have had this illustration of how you are treating yourself, trying stopping those thoughts in their tracks and replacing them with something more positive, or at least more compassionate.

One way of doing this is to visualise a big, red STOP sign every time you notice yourself putting yourself down or wallowing in misery. Choose a word or phrase that you associate with happy times, something funny: anything that will make you smile.

Have fun with this, you don't have to share it with anyone else so it can be as irreverent as you wish. Make a note of it in your notebook, though the idea is that it should be memorable.

My phrase is "magic days" – it never fails to lift my mood, make me pause, step back, remember that "this too shall pass." "Magic" reminds me of that childhood excitement and expectancy we were talking about earlier, of glorious sunsets and stunning harvest moons, of a brilliant magenta flower bud bursting out. "Magic days" emphasises to me that I will only live this particular day once, every moment of it is precious and deserves to be lived to its best.

It is also worth remembering that sometimes having compassion for ourselves may be allowing a time for a good cry or a wallow in self-pity. If possible choose the time and line up some things to help you afterwards, a good book, a treat, lunch with a friend (one with a positive disposition rather than one who will encourage you to continue wallowing). Emotions are there to be expressed not suppressed. Learning how to express them in a safe way for all concerned is a key part of developing emotional intelligence. Daniel Goleman and other writers have developed this into a whole area of study. There are some references at the end of this book to follow up if you wish to know more.

Exercise: Approaching change with compassion

If you already have some big changes planned, this exercise might be useful as a reminder where and when to remember to check if compassion is needed for yourself, and for other people around you.

Try this: take a new sheet of paper, on the left hand side write the heading "Change" and the date. Then two further headings: "Compassion: me" and "Compassion: others". (You may want to make more headings for individual people).

Underneath the heading "Change", list the things that are changing – whether under your control and planned or not. As you go, list how you need to show yourself compassion in relation to the changes, and what you can do for the others you have listed.

For example, if you are planning to become self-employed and start your own business, there will be all sorts of changes taking place: working hours;

41

how much you earn; becoming less (or maybe more) available for your family.

Once you have a good list, you could use them in a similar way to the "What" and "How" lists in Chapter 2. You can decide which actions you can take immediately, perhaps put them in order of priority, always remembering that you are as important as the other people in your life.

Chapter 6: Attention

A number of years ago I attended a seminar with Richard Wilkins (see References section for details of his books and website). He is an inspiring man with a talent for clear and simple communication. He speaks without notes and is full of energy and enthusiasm. I particularly remember the way he emphasised that "what you focus on becomes bigger and apparently more important."

I know when I spend time worrying about something it becomes bigger and bigger and more and more important in my mind. As a child and young person I could worry myself into a "tizzy" as my mother would call it. If she was late home I would convince myself she had been involved in some terrible accident. This certainly illustrates the power of our minds to physically affect our bodies – I would be feeling tense, jumpy, tearful, extremely stressed. And all about something that hadn't actually happened.

This is an extreme example of the negative self-talk we looked at in Chapter 5. Dwelling on past pains, hurt feelings and problems has a similar effect.

The Mark Twain quote mentioned earlier is also pertinent here: "I am an old man and have known a great many troubles, but most of them never happened."

And a more modern one: "Rule number one is, don't sweat the small stuff. Rule number two is, it's all small stuff." Robert Eliot. [4]

When we are caught up in the "drama" of our daily life it is easy to over-react and see everything as a crisis. This happens particularly when we are already over-stressed. The smallest thing can be the last straw and provoke an emotional reaction far bigger than the event itself warrants.

In the days before my diagnosis of cancer in 1994, I was under a lot of stress at work. At that time I ignored all the messages my body was trying to give me, and pushed myself harder and harder. I would cry and/or lose my temper at the smallest thing. I now know how to take notice of these messages before my health reaches such a breaking point.

Returning to Richard Wilkins, he wrote: "Miracles start to happen when you give as much energy to your dreams as you do to your fears."

---

[4] Both these from the website compilation on www.quotegarden.com

There is more in Chapter 9 on dealing with our fears and neutralising them by refusing to give them energy.

There are many books about the "law of attraction". (My personal favourite is *Life is a Gift* by Gill Edwards). My feeling is that nothing happens until you start moving yourself, starting to turn your thoughts into words, then words into actions in a deliberate and considered way. Simply wishing for something is unlikely to "attract" it to you, it is necessary for you to take some action too.

Richard Wilkins sends out occasional video messages. A while ago he sent a very funny one in which he demonstrated the law of attraction. He said he had decided to attract a pizza. He visualised it in technicolour detail, no pizza appeared. He imagined the smell and the taste (screwing his face up with the effort!). Still no pizza. He told the Universe how much he really, really wanted this pizza. Nothing. Eventually he picked up the phone, rang a number, and ordered his pizza.

Sometimes life really is this simple. If you want to meet people, go to places where those sorts of people go. If you want a new job, go out and look, get training that will help, actually apply for jobs.

Giving your attention to what you want makes it more likely that you will achieve it: taking action is what actually *makes* it happen!

Exercise: Where is your attention now?

Think about what you are focusing on right now. Take a few moments to write down all the things currently on your mind. Are they positive or negative? If they are negative, can you do anything to change them? If so, list some actions and either do something right away or make a note of when you will do so.

If you find you are dwelling on the past, think about how it is affecting your body and emotions. As well as worrying myself into a tizzy about something that hasn't happened, I am also an expert at dwelling on old hurts and making myself miserable all over again.

That is proof if I needed it of how I can create my reality, if I practise making myself feel good as often as I used to do the opposite I will soon be good at that too. (Getting better all the time!)

Chapter 7: Gratitude

A few years ago on the way home from work I went to visit my mother in the nursing home where she lived. She had been there since leaving hospital following a massive stroke. In one moment her life had changed from being an independent woman with many friends and interests to someone dependant on others for nearly everything.

That evening I went in as I did nearly every day, and after we had said hello, my mother said "I have been lying here counting my blessings, and the biggest one is you, Mary love." As you can imagine that had me on the verge of tears, and we shared a big hug (my mother could still do that very well even with only one working arm.)

It really brought home to me how much most of us take for granted all the good things in our lives. Most of us concentrate on things that are going wrong (giving our attention to those magnifies them as we discussed in Chapter 6), rather than what is going right.

Being grateful can take many forms: writing or thinking about a list is a starting point. As with all these exercises the feelings have to be real, genuine and actually *felt*. It won't be very helpful if you have a list of things you feel you *should* be grateful for. (Though if you find this is what you have, think through why those things are there, and some useful insights will arise.)

As with noticing your negative thoughts and changing them to positive ones (Chapter 5), working with gratitude lists is a technique that helps you develop new habits of thinking that can alter your attitude to the things that happen in your life. Simply write a list of things you are grateful for today, large and small. At this moment mine includes:

- the beautiful music I am listening to as I write
- the wild Cornish winter weather outside
- the luxury of sitting here at my desk writing.

Exercise: Making a gratitude list

- Write a gratitude list in your journal that you can look at whenever you wish
- When you go to bed at night think of three things to be grateful for that happened during the day.

This is a lovely thing to do with children at bedtime, it helps them get rid of worries and focus on a positive thought to take into sleep with them. It can also be an opening for talking about their day, especially useful for those children who do not normally share their thoughts and feelings.

Appreciation

Closely associated with gratitude is appreciation. Returning to the story at the beginning of this chapter about my mother's gratitude list on that day: she could have simply carried on thinking about her list to herself, that would have probably made her feel better and able to appreciate the things that were good about her life in spite of her situation.

However, the fact that she took the time to tell me how she felt made an enormous difference to me. How often do we tell people how much we appreciate them? Do you have memories of something that someone has said which has stayed with you?

A wonderful woman I know, Lizzie Fox, (www.beautifulpeopleimage.co.uk) is a very successful image consultant. During her talks to groups of women she urges everyone to tell their friends and people they come across when they look good, not in an insincere, falsely flattering way, but genuinely when they notice something.

Showing Appreciation

I have written to authors whose work has moved me in some way (so much easier to do now that most writers have websites) – and have been amazed sometimes to receive a reply saying how good it was for them to hear from a reader with positive feedback.

I know from my own experience how much difference that can make and how rarely it happens. My husband, Dave, was a lifeguard for many years and saved a number of people's lives over that time. In only one case did he get a real thank you, from an elderly man who gave him a now-treasured book with photos inserted of himself and my husband with an inscription that reads: "Dave Lunnen risked his life to save mine on Sunday July 11th 1976."

Appreciation is a way of passing on the good feelings you may get from feeling grateful, and sharing that warmth with others.

Sara Paddison, in her book *Hidden Power of the Heart* says: "The word 'appreciation' means to be thankful and express admiration, approval, or gratitude. It also means to grow or appreciate in value. As you appreciate life, you become more valuable - both to yourself and others."

Appreciation is expressing your gratitude, letting people know that something they have said or done has made a difference to you. A dear friend of mine who had been through some difficult times said to me a while later, "You have helped me such a lot, but you probably don't even know how."

I found that very moving and also literally empowering. It helped me recognise my own power as a person. Just going through life doing, and being, the best I can, had helped my friend, even when I may have thought to myself that I did not know what I could do for her. Often it is not the doing that makes the difference, it is the being: being with someone; spending time; being normal and treating them as normal too.

One of the stories my mother used to tell was that one day a woman she did not recognise came up to her in the street. She said she just had to say hello and thank my mother for something she had said a number of years earlier.

My mother had met her one day and, seeing she was obviously distressed, had asked if she could help. Out came the whole story: her son was being bullied at school and was extremely unhappy as he was about to move on to secondary school and the bullies would still be in the same class. In those days people automatically sent their children to the closest school, but my mother suggested that she simply ask if it was possible for him to attend a different school.

That was the end of the conversation and they never saw each other again until this occasion some years later. The woman said her son had been able to attend the other school, had been happy, had done extremely well in his studies and was now about to graduate from university.

The fact that this woman had taken the trouble to approach a stranger in the street – who, until she checked, she was not sure was the person she thought – and express her appreciation and gratitude for that brief conversation, made a huge difference to my mother. It was one of the things she remembered very clearly after her stroke and would tell as something that made her feel she had achieved useful things in her life. In Sarah Paddison's words, she had "become more valuable" both to herself and others.

I was very fortunate in that I was able to express my appreciation and gratitude to my mother before she died, something many people do not have the opportunity to do. How much better to practise the habit of doing this regularly for those we love and care for?

Exercise: Appreciation

Write a list of people you know: those very close to you, and those you may only have met a few times, or not seen for years, anyone that comes into your mind. People you live with; work with; teachers from years ago; someone who always serves you with a smile in your local shop or bank.

Next to their names, list the things that you appreciate about them. These might be big things, or small; something done over and over every day (the washing up perhaps!); a one off action that made a difference to your life, large or small.

Then write some actions for each one: send a card, letter or email; make a phone call; smile and say "thank you", really meaning it, to the bank teller; give your partner a big hug when they come in from work and tell them about the things you appreciate.

This may seem awkward at first but the rewards are immense: you will feel better for having expressed your appreciation and so will the people around you. You may find that they begin to express their appreciation of your actions also.

Chapter 8: Reconnection and dealing with feeling stuck

This chapter is a description of how I used a particular way of tackling my feeling of being stuck on one particular day. There are suggestions later for other approaches if this way is not for you.

Writing that day I just could not get started, my mind felt totally brittle, inflexible, as if it would break if I tried too hard. I felt disconnected: from myself; from any source of inspiration. So, I felt inclined not to write. But, after some thinking and reading I realised that this was what I needed to write about.

I was caught up in things about "me" – *I* wanted to finish this book, *I* was cross with *myself* for being stuck, *I* was irritated with the fact that my phone line was down due to storms.

So, after letting myself feel all these things, I decided to turn them around. No phone line, no email – what a fantastic opportunity to write without any interruptions or distractions! I wrote:

I am cross and irritated partly because it is cold and I am worried about paying the fuel bills and so I am skimping on heating in my office. Is that a good way to treat myself when I am trying to work productively? I now have a heater on and a nice hot cup of tea steaming in front of me.

Also, I am cross with myself because I have a pain in my ribs where I pulled a muscle in my yoga class last week. I have been attending the class for years and have very rarely had any sort of injury. It is "just" a pulled muscle that needs time to heal.

This morning I decided to write about this in my journal, and to use the technique of "asking" this pain in the ribs what it was trying to tell me. I wrote: "Please tell me what you are about." The "reply" was:

- tightness
- restriction
- something isn't right, it is sticking in, holding back
- pain of not breathing, not living *my* life – speak out!

My first reaction was "That's a bit 'deep' for a little strained muscle." (My pain in the rib's response was – "well, you asked!")

So then I asked: "How can I help you?" (the pain):

- rest
- relax
- talk to your husband, ask him for help

And: "How can you help me?"

- courage to speak up
- to realise how important this is
- support (just ask)

This all gave me a lot to think about and reflect on. Later I felt it was still too much on the surface, too much about my head not my heart, my ego not my higher self.

I turned to one of my library of books for some new insights: *Gulp* by Gabriella Goddard. I feel a real connection with Gabriella, she is from New Zealand where my sister and her family live and she has been inspired by many of the same writers and teachers I have come across. I have been dipping in and out of her book and each time I have found something of real value.

The section I was working on suggested visiting a creative place to open myself to new ideas and new views. I wasn't able to do this so decided instead to use some cards to prompt some new thoughts, and instead of my favourite angel cards, I got out my set of Hawaiian Oracle cards (by Rima Morrell).

The process took quite a while and was challenging and provoked new thinking particularly because the cards are not familiar. I asked for help with clearing the persistent block I have been feeling, not just in writing but in moving my coaching business forward and achieving financial success.

I wrote down my own responses to the three cards first, my reactions to what the animals pictured and their surroundings might signify for me. This deck puts a meaning on whether the cards are upright or reversed, and mine were all reversed. Perhaps this was an indication of how awkward I felt in my own life today. After I had thought about what I had written I read the interpretation in the book about each card, and wrote about how this felt to me and how it fitted with my own earlier responses. Some of the things I had written were similar to the book, others not.

Then I read through all the things I had written and reflected on what message I could draw from the words. I wrote down three key phrases:

- You are the architect of your own creativity
- Be open to all possibilities for your highest good and that of those around you
- Reconnect and get in touch with your dreams.

That was when I decided to write about this here to share with you. I felt that I had got away from my irritation with myself and concentration on material things. I had stepped away from my ego and towards the guidance of my higher self (intuition, subconscious) that is always there if we take time to still the mind and the "noise" around and inside our heads long enough to listen and really hear it.

I now want to write and reflect some more on those key phrases for myself and see where that leads me.

Exercise: Dealing with feeling stuck

If you are feeling stuck in some aspect of your life, you can tackle it in a similar way to my description above. You may feel that oracle or angel cards are not for you – perhaps reading at random from a favourite book of poetry works for you? Or physical activity: walking, gardening, dancing? Playing or listening to music? Painting, sewing, any sort of craft or arts activity? Anything that takes concentration and stops your internal self-talk for a while. Any of these can help you step away from the worries or concerns you are grappling with and make "space" for new inspiration to pop in from your unconscious, your higher self, whatever you like to call the source of your new ideas.

Some people find that asking a question last thing at night and asking for guidance can allow an answer to "pop into the mind" overnight whilst they are asleep.

Reading the stories of well-known entrepreneurs, you will find that many of them describe a breakthrough point in their businesses that occurred in such a way. Simon Woodroffe in *The Book of Yo!*, says about finding ideas: "Allow yourself some lazy time, whether it's in the garden, the bathtub or the car. Let your mind loose to fly."

Choose whatever works best for you, and record what happens in your journal if that is useful for you, to remember and develop the insights that arise.

Chapter 9: Fear

I have been concentrating on positive feelings (moving towards pleasure as discussed in the Introduction). Sometimes it is worth looking at the negatives as well to examine what is going on in order to move forward. Even though we use the words positive and negative which imply good and bad, everything has to have a balance, a shadow side if you like. There is no white without black, no day without night, no hot without cold, no yin without yang.

So, I feel that fear (like pain) can be a necessary ingredient: to prompt us to check; to prepare well; to plan; to train; to minimise risk. If not balanced by confidence fear can become paralysing. What stops most of us following our dreams and living a life we love? At the root of all the obstacles we face is fear.

People come to me with all sorts of issues they would like coaching to help them with. It could be a change of career; redundancy; loss of direction; relationship issues; finance; starting a business; wanting to get fit; recovering from illness or bereavement; low self-esteem – a huge range. As a coach I ask questions and help people really listen to their own answers. As we "drill down" to the underlying fundamentals usually "fear" is right at the core.

When we examine the evidence for our fears they are often unfounded, or exaggerated. Asking the question: "What is the very worst thing that could happen in this situation?" leads you to examine these fears and see that you have more strength and internal resources than you think to deal with whatever life brings.

For example, someone I worked with recently, (let's call her Simone), believed she couldn't afford to change her working hours to part time to start her own business doing something she really loved. The conversation involved me asking questions like: "What would have to be in place for you to feel able to go part time?", "How will you know when you have achieved this?", "What will it feel like when you achieve this?", "What would you do if there was no need to think about money?"

Simone's answers guided her through a process helping her to turn around her negative thinking ("I can't do this.") to a positive outlook ("I can do this, this way or this way.")

By the end of the first coaching session, Simone had decided on a series of practical actions, for example: work out a personal survival budget for the living expenses she had to cover each month; produce a business plan for her business with projected income figures in a cash flow forecast; approach her employer to initiate a discussion on part-time hours.

Over subsequent sessions we worked together to enable Simone to complete these actions and move forward in spite of her fears. Today she is running her business with energy and enthusiasm, and is negotiating with her employer to work for them on a freelance basis rather than set hours on a salary.

The Power of "Negative" thinking

I have a book by this title by Tony Humphreys, in which he argues that negative thinking is a protection for us: "protective thinking" rather than "negative thinking". An example is when people justify a pessimistic view of life by saying: "If

I don't expect anything good to happen, then I won't be disappointed."

In a similar way, Tony prefers to call positive thinking "open" thinking. He says: "..the label positive implies that it is the thinking which is the medium for change whereas it is the feelings with which it is infused that are the real source of power." The details of the book are in the 'References' section if you wish to read further on this. As we have already discussed, it is feelings not thoughts that have power to influence how we act, and fear is a very powerful feeling.

Like the shadow monster on the curtain we are frightened of as small children, we often have irrational fears that we hold without ever turning on a light and examining them to see exactly what they really are: if they have any substance at all.

Exercise: Tackle your fears

Try this: as with the "What?" and "How?" exercise in Chapter 2, start on the left hand side of a page with a list headed "Fears". Write down everything you can think of however silly it may sound to you. You may find that you only have a few main fears and that the other things you write could all be grouped under one heading (e.g. family member having an accident, someone close to you being ill). Leave room for three columns if you can (or you can simply follow on down the page instead).

In the middle column or below, write "Protects me from" and write something for each fear in your list. Next reflect on how real these fears are. It may be reasonable to be afraid of fast traffic on the road outside your house. Not so reasonable to worry about being hit by a falling asteroid.

Then choose which fears to tackle first and write about other ways of protecting yourself with actions rather than worrying. A fear is useful if it prompts you to take protective action. If you just worry more and more it becomes poisonous to you and self-destructive.

Take care not to let this exercise tempt you into a "wallowing in misery" session. Do it for as long as seems useful then choose some actions to go and do straight away. You may find this quite hard to do, and of course, as with any of these suggested exercises, you don't have to try it if it is not for you.

When I first had a go at this exercise I felt I was writing obvious things and couldn't really come up with good answers. I kept on writing the "silly" things down though, until I got to one that did make me think.

The fear was "that my business will fail." I wrote that this negative thought was protecting me from: "stepping out of my comfort zone." That felt significant to me: the fear of failure could be used as an excuse for not stepping out and trying new things.

The actions I decided to take were:

1. write and reflect more on this as it felt important to me.
2. revisit and update my business plan to put in some new activities that would challenge me to step out of my comfort zone, in a planned way (in thinking about this I realised I was already doing this but had not checked how the actions would fit with my plan, or if the plan needed revising).

So, even though I found it difficult at first I kept going and I allowed my thinking and writing to show me how best to proceed. I find this works for myself in my own personal development.

It is also how I work with my coaching clients: I ask them to tell me what works for them. If the answer is "I don't know.", we explore that through questions until something comes up. The guiding principle is that we all have the answers to our own questions within us, we just sometimes need a little help in finding them.

This chapter with the title "Fear" has been about dealing with it and moving on in spite of our fears. The classic book by Susan Jeffers *Feel the fear and do it anyway*, is a wonderful resource to use here. The sub-title says it all: "How to turn your fear and indecision into confidence and action."

My own book, *Flying in the Face of Fear*, shows how people just get on with it when faced with life-changing circumstances such as a diagnosis of cancer. The irony is that we seem often to be most indecisive just when the things we are dealing with are not of such great significance.

Examining our fears in a spotlight helps to distinguish the real from the unreal ones and frees energy to plan how to cope with those real ones in a way that can enable us to really overcome them rather than mentally sweep them under the carpet.

Chapter 10: Communication

The definitions of "communication" in the dictionary talk about "conveying information". For me it is about conveying *true* information, and we often do not ourselves know what is really the truth for us. We are so used to hiding what we really think and feel.

True communication would come straight from my heart to yours, I would be able to speak what was true for me in a way that would not hurt you even if it was not what you expected to hear. True communication is two-way – the person receiving it has to be open, clear and receptive too.

A lot has been written on communications styles, for example by Deborah Tannen (*You just don't understand: men and women in conversation.*) and John Gray (the *Mars and Venus* books). I don't believe it is just a male/female difference in style, (although this does have an effect). We all hear what we expect most of the time and don't listen fully. My husband frequently has to repeat something as I have not heard the first time round – I heard him speaking but being busy with something else have not actually *heard* what he said.

Some of us tend to speak in code and expect our companions to decipher this correctly. "Would you like to help by washing up?" from me would receive the logical answer "No, thank you" (i.e. they wouldn't "like" to). What I really mean of course is "Please will you wash up?"

If you would like to read more on this, see the books mentioned above. What interests me here is: how do we become clear ourselves on what we want to communicate? And then on how to make sure that the person receiving the message interprets it as we intend?

I sometimes think myself, and coaching clients often say, "I have no idea what I really want!" So how can we possibly ask other people to provide something for us if we do not know ourselves what it is? If you have tried some of the exercises earlier in this book you may have more clarity on this now. So, your Ideal Day piece might have given you some ideas. Your Vision Board has a clear picture of what you would like to see in your life soon. You may be able to use these to help you describe your dreams and goals to your family and others close to you.

Communicating clearly is a skill we begin to learn as a young child – remember how frustrated children can be when they know exactly what they want to say but cannot seem to make the adults around them understand? Once we are adults ourselves we may forget to keep practising and improving our communication skills, perhaps especially with those closest to us.

Communication has not happened until the person on the receiving end has heard and really understood the message you are intending to send. Just telling someone something does not mean they will immediately do as you ask. As in my example of the request to wash up – the listener may not understand that I was actually asking them to *do* the washing up unless I make it absolutely clear. (Of course they may choose to pretend not to understand, but that is another issue!)

Susan Scott, in her book *Fierce Conversations,* discusses how success can only be achieved "at work and in life, one conversation at a time." She describes techniques to help you become clear on what exactly you want to communicate. My coach recommended this book and I have found it extremely useful. If the concept inspires you I would urge that you look at the website and read the book (see References section).

One of Susan's suggestions is that it is worthwhile preparing for important conversations, whether they are at work or at home, in order to communicate clearly.

This is similar to writing down what you want to talk to your doctor about in order to be clear and not forget anything. I recently read[5] that doctors are trained to spot the last minute "and while I'm here, doctor" issue that a patient raises just as they get up to leave. This is often what is really troubling them.

The patient's communication, and therefore the service the doctor can give, would be much better if they had been focused and clear on what they wanted to say at the beginning of their appointment. To quote Susan Scott: "At the top of the appreciation list is the accurate identification of the problem."

Exercise: Clear communication
To help you in communicating clearly about a particular issue, try this exercise. It can be

---

[5] *How to get the best from your doctor* by Dr Tom Smith

undertaken in various ways: it could be a list down the page; a mind-map (see Tony Buzan, in References); using post-it notes or coloured cards. The key thing is to help you think clearly and constructively before opening a discussion.

There are a series of steps.

1. Define the issue you want to communicate: if you are not clear yourself, how can anyone else understand you? "Accurately identify" it as Susan Scott says. If you can do this clearly, when you do talk to the person it will help to reduce the risk of them becoming defensive: "You never help me with anything." is almost guaranteed to provoke a negative reaction, as it is almost certainly not true.

2. Write down why it matters to you. Also acknowledge how you may have contributed to the issue.

3. Decide what your ideal outcome would be.

4. List any alternative ways of achieving this outcome, including what you are already doing and plan to do in the future.

5. Decide what help you will ask for.

It may seem hard to practise an exercise on "communication" by yourself as by definition it has to involve more than one person. The process of reflection and becoming clear on exactly what the issue is, how you may have contributed to it and what you would like the outcome to be is extremely valuable, even before you get to the stage of talking to anyone else who may be involved.

Step 6 is where it moves on from being preparation. If you anticipate or assume what their answer will be you may firstly not approach them in the open way you intend, and secondly you may misinterpret their answer. So, having summarised your reflections above, you would ask the person directly for the help you need, and then really listen to their response, being prepared to hear what they say and talk through the options you have identified, together with any new suggestions they may have.

In my experience, people are pleased when someone takes the time and trouble to communicate clearly and this approach can resolve what might have seemed like impossible issues extraordinarily quickly. The focus must be on taking action once you have prepared. In the past I would run over various "scripts" in my head over and over again, falling into the trap of making assumptions of how the other person would respond. This would be the opposite of preparing well as I would be so worried and worked up by the time I spoke to the person that the words would come out wrong or I would get upset or angry.

A client, Sally, who was starting her own business, told me one day that she had booked an appointment with a competitor to find out more about how she ran her business. This is a valid way of undertaking market research, but she began to feel she was doing something underhand and became more and more worried about it.

The next time I saw her she was full of energy and enthusiasm, a different person. She told me she had got herself so "wound up" that she went bright red and blurted out the reason for her visit as soon as she arrived at the other person's premises. To her surprise her "competitor" was delighted that she was starting up in the area as she had far too much work and wanted to be able to refer some of her enquiries to another practitioner.

If Sally had not followed her instincts and been open she would probably not have learned of this valuable opportunity. She need not have undergone the mental torment in advance if she had not assumed that the other person's response would be hostile. She could have used the exercise above to prepare herself to be open.

I have only touched the surface of this subject here, there are all the issues of communication via the written word for example, especially when it is so easy now to send an email or text without really thinking about how it might be received at the other end.

As well as the words we use there are many other influences on how a listener receives a message: the context; tone of voice; body language. Think how many different ways of saying "yes" or "no" there are.

In addition to the impression given by the sender of the message, there are many factors concerning the receiver that also influence what is actually heard and understood. There may be cultural differences; the person may have physical issues: as well as being hard of hearing perhaps, there may be noise or distractions; they may be absorbed in their own thoughts and not really listening (the "yes dear" syndrome); they may be stressed or unwell.

To conclude this chapter, here are some thought-provoking (and some smile-inducing!) quotes (all from www.quotegarden.com):

"The trouble with talking too fast is you may say something you haven't thought of yet." (Ann Landers.)

"The real art of conversation is not only to say the right thing at the right place but to leave unsaid the wrong thing at the tempting moment." (Dorothy Nevill.)

"Be careful of your thoughts; they may become words at any moment." (Ira Gassen.)

"The difference between a smart man and a wise man is that a smart man knows what to say, a wise man knows whether or not to say it." (Frank M. Garafola.)

"I just wish my mouth had a backspace key." (Author unknown.)

Chapter 11: Aspirations

In this chapter, I want to think about aspirations. Not vision or goals or objectives or ambitions. Aspiration to me means something I aspire to. The dictionary definition of this is "to have ambitions to do or be something." For me this is to be the best, greatest, fullest most wonderfully blossoming person I can possibly be.

Just because I am human and cannot be my best all the time does not mean I should not aspire to be so. In any case, "being my best" is just that, being my best in any particular situation.

If I am feeling tired, run-down and dispirited, my best might be to take myself away from other people to rest and regain my energy and inspiration. Doing that best would mean doing it in a way that honours my own needs, not feeling guilty for looking after myself. And at the same time being clear and fair with the people around me.

Being my best also means being realistic, and still stretching myself to achieve more. Not being such a perfectionist that I never finish anything.

Knowing when I have achieved my best in a situation and knowing when to leave it and move on.

It means holding big ambitions for myself, allowing myself to truly believe I am capable of great things, stretching my comfort zone and surprising myself. Daring to shine my light and not hide it under a bushel. We are all unique human beings with special gifts to offer.

Exercise: Acting on your aspirations

Start by flow writing for five minutes about this, and then pick out the key phrases. In my example above I picked up on "being my best" and thought and wrote about that a little.

Look back at all the things you have done in the past and congratulate yourself on your achievements. Look at any of the exercises you have done from this book – perhaps your vision board or writing about your ideal day.

Write down the key things that you aspire to achieve and then think about how you can make a start on doing them. What one action can you take today or tomorrow to take the first step?

It may not be on the scale you would like immediately, for example helping bring peace to the world. In what small ways can you promote that grand vision? It might be campaigning or politics or volunteering abroad. It might be working in a hospice or a homeless shelter or donating part of your salary. It might be making an effort to get on with a neighbour. There will be something you can do that will make a difference, however small.

Full circle

We have come back full circle to where we began, looking at what we want and how to do it – and taking action. I am writing this in the last days of December, looking back at the year just ending and forward to the new one about to start. I believe life is full of circles and cycles, nothing is linear or fixed. Everything changes, moves on, dies and is reborn.

My hopes for you are that you will have enjoyed reading this book and will read more, (from the references or the wealth of other books available), as the inclination takes you, along your own special and individual path. I wish you joy, happiness and satisfaction from whatever comes next in your life and I hope to cross paths again with you again at some time, whether this be through the written word such as this or in person through coaching calls, workshops, or emails.

Before moving on to "What Next?", it feels appropriate to share the words of the Serenity Poem:

God grant me the serenity to accept the things
I cannot change,
the courage to change the things that I can,
and the wisdom to know the difference.
(Reinhold Niebuhr)

Chapter 12: What next?

I hope that you have enjoyed reading this book. If you have tried any of the exercises, they may have led you to some useful insights. You may wish to explore further and follow-up by reading some of the books listed in the References section. Most of the authors will have websites which will include information on their other publications, newsletters, workshops and talks.

If you would like to experience one-to-one life coaching do some research and choose a life coach whose style appeals to you and give it a try. Perhaps talk to more than one coach. It is a very personal relationship that involves trust, so you must be totally at ease and comfortable with the coach you choose in order to get the best from your coaching. Most coaches offer a free consultation so you can find out if their style is right for you.

Writing and using journals in coaching

You might also want to continue using your notebook as a reflective journal to record your experiences, thoughts and feelings. I use journals and

81

other writing in a professional capacity in my work as a life coach, business adviser and trainer. I encourage my clients and students to become aware of the way their thoughts can affect their reality and of how useful it is to step back from the immediate day-to-day business of life and reflect.

Some people are not naturally drawn to writing down their thoughts: sometimes other techniques are more helpful for them. Visual activities can be very effective, such as using colours to express a vocabulary of emotions instead of words. Collages such as the vision board are a great tool as well. Mind-mapping is another technique that frees the mind from the traditional linear list-making structure. (This was developed by Tony Buzan, and he has published many books and articles on the subject).

My clients often invent their own ways of working: one person dealt with time-management by putting all her daily tasks onto coloured cards and making a game of turning them over in order to choose where to start and who in the household would take on each task. Others use coloured post-it notes to organise their thoughts.

The pieces of impromptu artwork that people attending the Dare to Blossom workshops create hold great significance and important stories for their makers. Anna Colmer, quoted earlier, has written a piece for my website on the significance of her "Medusa" for her.

"When Mary asked us to create something from the materials she'd provided, I found myself very drawn to the mass of coloured wools. I began to pick out the colours that appealed - blues, greens, greys and turquoise - sea colours. The images of seaweed, sea serpents and then snakes followed in quick succession, then the image of Medusa, with serpents for hair.

This image resonated deeply with me as one of the issues I'd brought to the workshop was getting in touch with my creativity. Medusa seems to me to be a negative and destructive feminine archetype - she turns all who look on her to stone. Consequently, she is isolated and shunned. She is out of touch with the free-flowing, creative energy, the generative quality which is also part of the feminine birthright.

She represents the sterility of being cut off from that creative impulse. Medusa's physical form came together very quickly for me once I'd identified her. Her face was inspired by the masks worn by the chorus in traditional Greek theatre and I felt pleased when another participant said 'oh, it's a Greek mask', when I held up my finished work. Her expression is a mournful one and also hints at resentment and bitterness. She is both feared and vilified by others, a creature who knows only how to destroy. She is frozen at her core and unable to grow.

I feel enormously fond of Medusa although she represents such a negative image and it is richly ironic that I have connected more deeply with my creative potential in making her. She is what we could all become if we lose touch with our creative energy. I keep her near my desk, where I can see her gloomy countenance every day and she makes me smile. She is a reminder to me to stay in touch with my playful, spontaneous, creative instincts, as I don't wish to become her!"

Thank you Anna, and to all my clients, and people I have met along the way, for inspiring me.

I have been challenged by a wise and perceptive friend to write more about my own process of "Daring to Blossom", and have started planning another book that will tell this story. In the meantime the Postscript that follows contains a brief account of my path to this point.

Postscript: From cancer to coaching

In May 2004 I wrote an update to send out with copies of *Flying in the Face of Fear* on the tenth anniversary of my cancer diagnosis. It is now (January 2008 at the time of writing) nearly fourteen years on and people are again asking me "what happened next?" How I did I travel a path "from cancer to coaching"?

That first book grew out of the journal I began on the day of my diagnosis. I knew with absolute certainty that I had to write about what I was going through: for myself, not for anyone else. What I wrote was not written for publication: it was rambling complaints; worries; sometimes "what I did today" particularly in relation to the treatment I received for my illness.

It was sometimes therapeutic, I found it vital to have a place to work through my thoughts and feelings about what was happening to me, to make sense of them. I felt I couldn't express all of my fears with anyone, I felt I had to protect my family and friends, be strong for them.

As Natalie Goldberg says in *Writing Down the Bones*, I "wrote through my pain, tried to write it out and let it go." My GP referred me to the Community Psychiatric Nurse (the closest they had to a counsellor at my surgery then). I did not find it at all helpful at that time, just a few days after my diagnosis. I did see a counsellor some years later and found it very useful for a short time to deal with specific issues.

So, I just wrote and wrote and filled a number of notebooks (the number is still growing 14 years on). A few years later I decided to use my experiences to help other women and their families, so I began compiling a book of women's stories of cervical cancer, including my own.

It was an incredible experience, the women I spoke to had been through so much and their writing was so strong, honest, practical, moving, and funny. One contributor called her chapter "Tumour Humour". I remember a local radio interviewer being quite shocked by that, then getting the point – we have to use humour in difficult situations.

I continued to write in my journal every day and that practice has helped me through subsequent difficult events in my life. For many years after my treatment for the cancer – a radical hysterectomy – I suffered severe post-operative pain. For some time this had huge effects on my life reaching into every area – work, my relationship with my husband, my ability to spend time with friends, to travel and even to walk far.

Although the doctors never found an explanation satisfactory to me, it has gradually lessened over the years and now hardly affects me at all. However, I still find myself surprised and shocked every so often when it returns suddenly. Now my reaction is to rest, and to write: I have several pieces written to help me understand; to "ask" the pain why it is here; what I need to learn from it. Usually it is my body "shouting" at me to stop, rest, slow down.

New directions

In April 1999 I took a job as research assistant with Cornwall Community Health Council, becoming part of a small team of staff supporting a board of voluntary members with the remit of being the "Patient's Watchdog".

I had just settled into that role when in July 2000 the NHS Plan was published and the abolition of the CHCs in England was included. "Announced" is not the right word as the first the staff knew of it was reading the Plan when it was published on the Internet. In the event, the abolition process took until December 2003, during which time the Cornwall CHC continued with normal work on behalf of patients as long as possible, but the last few months were a sad process of closing down and hunting for jobs.

Discovering the value of life coaching

During this time the NHS provided counselling for staff but not life coaching. I found a coach, Fraser Dyer, through a recommendation in a newsletter and began self-funded telephone sessions with him. I found this hugely useful, particularly in the difficult situation of only qualifying for redundancy payments after a long and distressing search for "suitable alternative employment" within the NHS.

I experienced the extraordinary situation of being given negative feedback on an interview as the prospective employer had to justify not appointing an "at risk" (of redundancy) person such as myself, by explaining why I was not good enough. Fraser was a great support during this time, encouraging me to recognise that I always had choices; that I could look outside the tunnel vision encouraged by this process.

I continued to be involved with Cancerbackup, reviewing patient information booklets prior to publication, and with Macmillan Cancer Support, working for a while as a trainer on occasional courses for support groups.

Before leaving the CHC I began a part-time job as business adviser and trainer with a local college, a totally new area of work for me, and one which involved a lot of new learning.

At the same time I was studying to become a life coach. My experience of the coaching process with Fraser had shown me how it fitted into the personal development workshops I had written and delivered for local adult education and the work I had done in training with Macmillan. I knew it was a way of working with people I would love and be able to use all my experience to be good at doing.

Other health scares

Although I started "journaling" seriously in 1994, I have always written, from my childhood love of stories and letter writing, to academic work, research reports, business writing. It was much more than the basis of my story of my cancer experience that I included with those of the other women in *Flying in the Face of Fear.*

After my fiftieth birthday I had my first mammography screening, and to my horror was recalled for further investigations and a biopsy. Even though the doctor assured me that it was just a routine precaution to look at a shadow, all the feelings of fear and panic that I felt on hearing the cancer diagnosis years earlier came flooding back.

The seven days wait for the results seemed more like seven weeks, but all was well when they came. As happened after the surgery for my cervical cancer, I suffered from pain in the area of the biopsy for some time and had to return for a follow-up to check on the cause of this but no explanation was found. (I think now I must simply be very sensitive to pain.)

Without perhaps realising it, a key part of my personal identity became "writer", it is who I am, what I do. So when, in 2002 I developed severe pain in both wrists it was devastating. I could not type or write with a pen without suffering badly. It was diagnosed as tenosynovotis (inflammation of the tendon sheaths) combined with osteo-arthritis in my joints.

I still wrote briefly in my journal, I felt I had to, though looking back there are some weeks with no entries at all. My left wrist was not quite as painful so I tried writing with that hand, very shakily. I felt the core of my being was under threat and I wrote "I feel as if I am losing my 'voice'."

I received some treatment that helped and some that didn't. I developed tactics for computer use, such as using more shortcuts instead of the mouse. I still have to be very careful about position and about over-use of my wrists. What I have learnt is just how important it is to me to be able to express myself in words, and that it can be done without writing: by speaking, recording.

And that I can express myself in other ways through art and creative activities. And most of all how to still find my identity: although an important part of that is to do with writing, that label of "writer" is not who I am. I am a unique human being with a whole range of talents and ways of communicating.

My journal has become a lifetime companion

As well as helping me cope with my own illnesses, my journal has been an essential companion to me during other life events. In 1999 my mother, previously an active and independent woman, suffered a severe stroke. I found her after she had lain on the floor of her house for 24 hours, unable to summon help.

The first few days were very hard, not knowing how she had been affected, if she would be able to talk, if her understanding or memory would be gone. After a few days, she gestured for a pen and paper – a precious miraculous moment, the power of the written word marking such a hugely important breakthrough. One of the things she wrote was "go home and rest" – still my dear mother looking after me! She could not speak (or swallow) because the muscles in her throat had been affected. She later recovered the power of speech and most, though not all, of her mental capacity.

So, I wrote all through the years after this: through finding my mother a nursing home; helping her cope with the huge changes to her life; through selling her house to pay the fees, first having the privilege of sitting with her sorting through family photos and mementos; through having to find a new home for her when the place where she was settled closed with only four weeks notice.

Finally, in 2005, after various other illnesses and accidents that reduced her quality of life even more, I was with my mother as she gave up on life, looking forward to the release of death. I was there when she begged that the doctor be allowed to give her something "to put me out of my misery", which of course he was unable to do. And finally I was there too, with my brother, when she breathed her last breath and passed on.

Good times as well as bad

I haven't listed these events to relive the pain and sorrow or to ask for your sympathy. I know that this tale of mine is just life as it is lived by everyone. Everyone has sad events in some form. For me that is when I turn to my journal to "write them out". It is how many of us cope with events that are significant to us as individuals and I have found that my use of my journal has been an integral part of my personal growth during these years.

I have also chronicled the joyous times: the birth of my great nephews and nieces; celebrations of anniversaries; my pleasure in the wonderful place in Cornwall where I live. I record small reflections and observations on the passing seasons in my garden. I record in my 'gratitude' list all the things, large and small that make me glad to be alive and glad to be me.

My journal sometimes includes fragments of poetry and pieces of writing that I use later for articles or newsletters. It is a friend I turn to, where I can be myself, and where I can find myself again in times of change. Writing has been a constant companion on my path "from cancer to coaching". It will continue to be one of the tools I use to make sense of the events in my life and their effects on me.

I am also realising that there are many other routes to self-awareness and personal development, such as yoga, meditation, art and all sorts of creative activity. Sometimes these enable a deeper connection than that which comes through "brain work", so they work together in harmony with my writing.

This is the beginning of my next phase of daring to blossom, stepping up to be my true self and expressing that openly in my life, my work and my writing. I will be responding to my friend's words: "Dare to be you, stop hiding behind the coaching, and then challenge the readers to dare to be themselves and really amp up the energy both in yourself and in them." So – look out for the next book!

An invitation to you

I would love to hear from you with feedback on the book and to answer any questions you may have about coaching. Contact me on 01841 540552, 07778 771021, mary@daretoblossom.co.uk or visit www.daretoblossom.co.uk.

List of exercises

References and Resources

Most of the authors listed here will have websites which contain details of other publications, opportunities to sign up for newsletters and other information about their work.

Carol Adrienne: The purpose of your life
Thorsons, 1998 ISBN 0-7225-3727-1
www.caroladrienne.com

William Bloom: Feeling Safe
Piatkus, 2002 ISBN 0-7499-2371-7
www.williambloom.com

Tony Buzan: Mind Maps at Work
Thorsons, 2004 ISBN0-00-715500-X
www.buzanworld.com

Julia Cameron: The Artist's Way - A course in discovering and recovering your creative self.
Pan Books, 1995 ISBN 0330-34358-0
www.theartistsway.com

Neil Crofts: Authentic – how to make a living by being yourself.
Capstone, 2003 ISBN 1-84112-519-9
www.authentictransformation.co.uk

Fraser Dyer: Why do I do this every day? Finding meaning in your work.
Lion, 2005 ISBN 0-7459-5171-6
www.myworkinglife.com

Gill Edwards: Life is a Gift
Piatkus, 2007 ISBN 978-0-7499-2781-3
www.livingmagically.co.uk

Viktor E Frankl: Man's Search for Meaning
1985, Washington Square Press ISBN 0-671-02337-3

Gabriella Goddard: Gulp.
Penguin, 2006 ISBN 0-141-02528
www.gabriellagoddard.com

Natalie Goldberg: Writing down the bones
Shambhala, 1986, 2005 ISBN 1-59030-316-4
www.nataliegoldberg.com

Daniel Goleman: Emotional Intelligence
Bantam Dell, 1996 ISBN 0-553-840070
www.danielgoleman.info

John Gray: Venus and Mars series
www.marsvenus.com

Fiona Harrold: Be your *own* life coach
Coronet, 2001 ISBN 0-340-77064-3
www.fionaharrold.com

Louise L Hay: You can heal your life
Eden Grove Editions, 1996 IBSN 1-870845-21-8
www.louisehay.com

Michael Heppell: How to be Brilliant!
Pearson Education, 2004, ISBN 0-273-67582-6
www.michaelheppell.co.uk

Napoleon Hill: 'Think and Grow Rich',
www.naphill.org

Robert Holden: Happiness now!
Hodder & Stoughton, 1998 ISBN 0-340-71308-9
www.happiness.co.uk

Robert Holden: Shift Happens!
Hodder & Stoughton, 2000 0-340-71688-6
www.happiness.co.uk

Tony Humphreys: The Power of 'Negative' Thinking
Newleaf, 1996 ISBN 0-7171-3004-5
www.tonyhumphreys.ie

Susan Jeffers: Feel the fear and do it anyway.
Vermilion. Latest reprint 2004 ISBN 0-7126-7105-6
www.susanjeffers.com

Elizabeth Mapstone: Stop dreaming, start living
Vermilion, 2004 ISBN 0-0918-9461-1
www.elizabethmapstone.co.uk

Susan Mitchell: Be Bold!
Simon & Schuster, 2000 ISBN 0-7318-0495-3

Maria Nemeth: The Energy of Money
Random House, 1997, 1999 ISBN 0-345-43497-8
www.marianemeth.com

Sarah Paddison: Hidden Power of the Heart
Planetary (date unknown) ISBN 187905243-1

Rima Morrell: The Hawaiian Oracle, 2006,
Connections Publishing ISBN 1-85906-202-4
www.hunalight.com

Ben Renshaw: Successful but something missing
Rider, 2000 ISBN 0-7126-7053-X

Jack Russell: Don't tell the Bumblebee
PDC Inspiration, 2006 ISBN 0-9553447-0-0
www.pdcinspiration.com

Dr Tom Smith: How to get the best from your
doctor, Sheldon Press 2007 ISBN 978-1-84709-007-2

Susan Scott: Fierce Conversations
Piatkus, 2002 ISBN 0-7499-2381-4
www.fierceinc.com

Deborah Tannen: You just don't understand.
Virago, 1991, ISBN 1-85381-471-7

Kathy Tyler and Joy Drake: The Angel Cards Book
Narada Productions 1999 ISBN 0-934245-41-X
www.innerlinks.com

Marian Van Eyk McCain: The Lilypad List
Findhorn Press, 2004 ISBN 1-84409-037-X
www.lilypadlist.com

Neale Donald Walsch: Conversations with God
(series) www.nealedonaldwalsch.com

Richard Wilkins: Mental Tonic
Cantecia, 1998 ISBN 0-9528-1988-0
www.theministryofinspiration.com

Nick Williams: The work we were born to do
Element, 1999 ISBN 1-86204-552-6
www.nick-williams.com

Barbara J. Winter: Making a Living without a Job
Bantam, 1993 ISBN 0-553-37165 7
www.barbarawinter.com

Simon Woodroffe: The Book of Yo!
Yo How! 2004 (second edition) ISBN 0-9547566-0-6
www.yosushi.com

Milton Keynes UK
Ingram Content Group UK Ltd.
UKHW011359120724
445582UK00033B/457